MW00954171

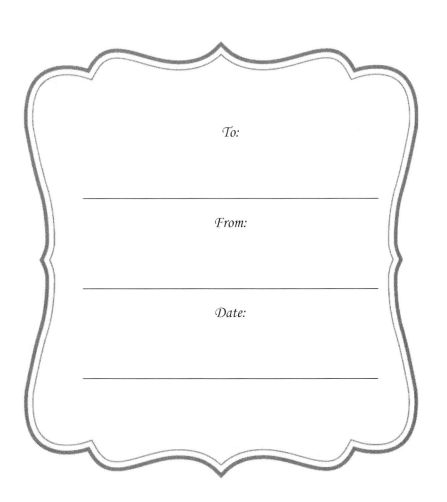

To:

From:

Date:

ChiselBooks

USA

Introduction

When Thomas Paine penned *Common Sense* it changed the mindset of the colonist people of America. This persuasive argument is credited with swaying public opinion in favor of separating from Great Britain, an act from which the United States of America was born.

Words convince and sway. They can be used to create or to destroy. God created the universe and everything in it, just by speaking the words. Jesus often healed with just a command. The Bible itself is a collection of words, but it changed the world. Greek philosophers understood the existential essence of "word" as a force. They called it "logos," an idea that encompassed thought, philosophy, and expression. Words were more than just a communication tool. For the Greeks, "word" was the essence of existence.

That's what John was communicating when he said, "In the beginning was the Word, and the Word was with God, and the Word was God" (John 1:1). He went on to define Jesus as the Word that became flesh (John 1:14), meaning Jesus was the embodiment of the old and new covenants, perfection wrapped up in humanity. To be with Jesus is to read the books of God's law and love.

It is because words have such influence over the heart and mind that *Write God in Deeper* can effectively guide Christian women into a richer faith. Through encouragement and a series of journaling prompts, each chapter provides tools for meditation, study, and daily application. Your faith will benefit from in-depth concentration on 25 key biblical traits that will enrich your experience in the abundant life and create a lasting effect on others around you.

Nancy was concerned she didn't have a "relationship" with God. After all, a relationship required time, and she never spent time with God. Nancy didn't know how to have the spiritual life she saw in other Christian women. With small children and teenagers at home, how could she find the time to pray, read her Bible, and meditate?

Perhaps you find yourself in a similar life stage. Schedules seem busier than ever. Laundry and grocery shopping are hard to catch up on, let alone Bible reading. Even this book was a stretch in your already busy, guilt-ridden life. Still, something in your soul craves that relationship, and it keeps you searching for the time to indulge.

The longing you feel is like spiritual hunger pangs. Jesus said you cannot live by meeting your physical needs alone. You have to feed the spiritual (Matthew 4:4). He also said, "… Apart from me you can do nothing" (John 15:5). The longing to spend time with God in His word isn't an indulgence. It's breath, food, water, and shelter. You take time to eat, drink, and rest your body. Your spirit needs it even more.

But how? That's the real question, isn't it? Nancy discovered a couple of secrets that can help.

First, she asked God to give her a heart for His word. God said, "Call to me and I will answer you …" (Jeremiah 33:3). If you ask God to give you the desire to be with Him, He will give it to you.

Second, Nancy learned to ignore false guilt. She said, "I just stopped worrying about what needed to be done and took time for God anyway." Nancy discovered all the work she thought she wouldn't have time to do, somehow got done.

In the Bible, sisters Martha and Mary were close friends with Jesus. Once, when Jesus came over for a gathering, Martha bustled around while Mary sat at His feet. How do you think Jesus responded? "Martha, Martha, you are anxious and troubled about many things, but one thing is necessary. Mary has chosen the good portion which will not be taken away from her" (Luke 10:41-42). Put God first, and He'll take care of the rest.

Read the story of Mary and Martha recorded in Luke 10:38-42.

How does this story encourage and challenge you?

Read Jesus's teaching about daily worries recorded in Matthew 6:25-34.

How does this resonate in your life?

_____

_____

_____

_____

_____

_____

_____

_____

_____

_____

_____

_____

_____

_____

_____

_____

_____

_____

_____

_____

_____

_____

_____

English clergyman William Gurnall said, "Pray often rather than very long at a time. It is hard to be very long in prayer, and not slacken in our affections." Prayers don't have to be long to be effective.

Consider ways you can pray short sincere prayers throughout the day.

Think about your regular schedule. Are you too busy to spend time with God?

If so, what are some activities you can cut out?

Consider the habits and activities you feel you can't live without. How do you make time for those?

How can you sacrifice in order to make time for your spiritual life?

Ed Cole, founder of The Christian Men's Network, said, "Wishing will never be a substitute for prayer."

What do you think is the difference between wishing and praying?
How does this challenge your perspective?

_____

_____

_____

_____

_____

_____

_____

_____

_____

_____

_____

_____

_____

_____

_____

_____

_____

_____

_____

_____

_____

_____

_____

Sometimes we don't know what to say to God, and we don't have to. Consider the words of Charles Stanley: "Often times God wants us to sit before Him in quietness. He doesn't want us to do all the talking. Isaiah 30:15 says, 'In quiet and confidence will be your strength'" (KJV). God wants to listen and spend time with you.

To represent His presence, put an empty chair in front of you and talk to God one-on-one. Write down what He says to you.

Maltbie Babcock was a Presbyterian minister and writer of the beloved hymn, "This is My Father's World." Babcock was known for his passionate faith and love of nature. He would often steal away just to watch birds in a meadow. He once said, "This is the best possible world for one who is called according to God's purpose … Can we imagine a world better fitted for those ends …? How long are we to suffer or to serve is for God to say. Let us not look … too impatiently at the clock. When God's time for us comes, well and good. Till then, this world is best for us, and we must make the most of it and do our best for it."

Babcock understood God created this life to be enjoyed. Yes, there are times of suffering and labor, but there is still so much to delight in. When mankind sinned, God could have taken away all beauty and serenity on earth to curse them. He could have made the world a desolate place, but He didn't. He allowed us to experience a full, beautiful life.

Jesus said, "I came that they may have life and have it abundantly" (John 10:10). When God gives, He gives generously and completely. When we abide in Christ, connected to Him through prayer, praise, and the Word, we benefit from the flow of His goodness. Psalm 1:1-3 describes the life of a believer like "a tree planted by streams of water that yields its fruit in its season, and its leaf does not wither. In all that he does, he prospers."

The fullness of life shouldn't be confused with earthly gain of wealth and prosperity. We should always give thanks for physical blessings, and we should honor God by giving generously. But the gifts that make life abundant are far greater than earthly possessions. Joy, purpose, and contentment are treasures money cannot buy. They are free to all who follow Christ.

Rather than focusing on trials and troubles, we should ask God for a spirit of gratitude and contentment. We can give praise in the midst of darkness, and give thanks in times of peace. To enjoy the gifts of God is to have pleasure in Him, and nothing pleases God more.

Ask God to open your eyes to the good in every day.

Write down some of the wonderful gifts that God gave you this week.

What are the ways God has blessed you abundantly? Are you blessed with resources, money, talents?

How can you give to others from the abundance God has given you?

Jesus said, "… Give, and it will be given to you. Good measure, pressed down, shaken together, running over, will be put into your lap. For with the measure you use it will be measured back to you" (Luke 6:38).

How do Jesus's words challenge and inspire you?

John MacArthur, Bible teacher and scholar, wrote, "People who truly desire God's blessing must resist the devil and his schemes. That means before we have a right to expect God to bless us, we must turn away from the evil that hinders that blessing."

How does MacArthur's comment apply to your life?

William Gurnall said, "Truly the saint's heaviness reflects unkindly upon God Himself. We do not commend His cheer if it does not cheer us."

What if people knew God only by the way you reflect Him in your attitude about life? How would they describe Him?

"[The rich] are to do good, to be rich in good works, to be generous and ready to share, thus storing up treasure for themselves as a good foundation for the future, so that they may take hold of that which is truly life" (1 Timothy 6:18-19).

How can you be rich in good works?

Follow the lead of Maltbie Babcock and spend some time in nature.

What are the different ways you see God's blessings?

The song "Belong," by Chris Rice, tells the story of a wounded orphan, lost and alone in the woods. The child explains:

Fading memories ignored, I crawl across the forest floor.
Pool reflects an orphan child, dirty, lost, alone and wild.
Fatherless and nameless still. Fallen heart and broken,
Will there ever be a place where I belong?

Perhaps you, too, have wondered where you belong. People may surround you, yet you feel outcast and misunderstood. You long to be known, loved, and accepted just as you are. Maybe you go to church, but sometimes you feel judged there. Maybe it's hard to witness the loving, caring families, because your own family is so different. You may wonder if God can really love a person with such dark secrets. Are you good enough for Him?

I have good news. Belonging is attainable, but you won't find it in any place, not even church. That yearning was put in you by your Creator who desires a relationship with you, and it can only be filled by spending time with Him.

The truth is, none of us are good enough, but that's exactly why Jesus came—to give us a way to know God deeply and intimately, despite our faults! God doesn't need you to be pure or perfect. You can come just as you are, and He will cleanse you.

Because of Jesus, we are adopted by God as His children. He chose us, and we carry His name. God said, "Fear not, for I have redeemed you; I have called you by name, you are mine." (Isaiah 43:1). Not only that, but Revelation 2:17 says God will give us a special name, known only by the one to whom it is given. Could it be God's pet name for each of His children? How is that for intimacy and belonging?

There is only one way to achieve intimacy with God—talking to Him in prayer and reading His love letter—the Bible. Try it and see what it feels like to come "home."

The Bible says we are chosen (1 Peter 2:9). God didn't get "stuck" with any of His children. We are His because He wanted us to be His.

How does this make you feel?

_____

_____

_____

_____

_____

_____

_____

_____

_____

_____

_____

_____

_____

_____

_____

_____

_____

_____

_____

_____

_____

_____

_____

_____

Jesus said God knows when every sparrow falls (Matthew 10:29). God collects our tears in a bottle (Psalm 56:8), and He counts every hair on our heads (Matthew 10:30).

If God knows you better than you know yourself and He still loves you, what does this say about God's love for you?

Henry Martyn, missionary to India, said, "I am born for God only. Christ is nearer to me than father, or mother, or sister—a nearer relation, a more affectionate friend; and I rejoice to follow Him, and to love Him. Blessed Jesus! Thou art all I want—a forerunner to me in all I ever shall go through as a Christian, a minister, or a missionary."

How can you relate to these words?

John and Stasi Eldredge wrote in their book *Captivating,* "We cannot have intimacy with God or anyone else if we stay hidden and offer only who we think we ought to be or what we believe is wanted."

How have you been hiding yourself?

The book *Revelations of Divine Love* explains the unconditional love and acceptance of God. It says, "It is very greatly pleasing to [God] that a simple soul should come naked, openly, and familiarly."

How can you come naked and open to God?

Write about times you felt rejected or outcast by friends or loved ones. Then offer this list to God as a sacrifice.

Write a prayer asking God to reveal His unconditional acceptance to you.

What are ways you have felt rejected by the church?

Write a prayer asking God to cover each of these times with grace and for the strength to forgive.

"I heard a trumpet," Anna said. She and her kids were headed inside at the end of a long, cool evening. Everything was eerily quiet, and then she heard a hollow blow not once, but twice. "It was so strange. I had no idea where it came from, but all I could think was, 'Is Jesus coming?' For days I kept an eye on the sky."

Jesus didn't come back that day, but Anna was ready. She remembered the words of her Savior, "Therefore, stay awake, for you do not know on what day your Lord is coming" (Matthew 24:42). Rev. Matthew Henry wrote, "As Christians, we profess, not only to believe and look for, but to love and long for, the appearing of Christ … The second coming of Christ is the center in which all the lines of our religion meet, and to which the whole of the divine life hath a constant reference and tendency."

Christians are called to act as if Jesus is coming today. We are to look for Him to return, just as He said He would. Even if He doesn't return in our lifetime, it isn't extreme or strange to hope and look. Jesus said His coming would be like a thief in the night for those who aren't ready, but the watchful won't be taken by surprise. Paul said, "… You are not in darkness, brothers, for that day to surprise you like a thief" (1 Thessalonians 5:2-4).

But how do we remain watchful? Jesus told a parable of ten virgins who were waiting for their bridegroom (Matthew 25:1-13). Five had oil in their lamps, and five did not. When the bridegroom came, only the five with oil were ready. Oil is often a symbol of the Holy Spirit or the anointing of God. Would you describe your life as filled with the anointing of the Holy Spirit?

Paul admonishes us not to "quench the Spirit" (1 Thessalonians 5:19). We must keep filled with the Word, prayer, praise, and meditation until God answers our prayers, and we finally see His face.

Jesus said, "Therefore, stay awake, for you do not know on what day your Lord is coming" (Matthew 24:42).

How do you "stay awake" in your daily life?

Jesus tells the church in Revelation 3:2, "Wake up, and strengthen what remains and is about to die, for I have not found your works complete in the sight of my God."

If Jesus said this to the people of your church, what would you do?

"Continue steadfastly in prayer, being watchful in it with thanksgiving."
(Colossians 4:2).

Write a prayer that is watchful and full of thanks.

Max Lucado wrote, "We are too content. We seldom watch the skies. We rarely run to the temple. We seldom, if ever, allow the Holy Spirit to interrupt our plans and lead us to worship so that we might see Jesus."

Imagine the day Jesus returns. What will it look like to see Him in all His glory?

Pastor Ken Hutcherson said, "We have no business letting the world get us down. When I start feeling down, I turn to the last chapter of the book of Revelation. There is no way I can ever, ever stay down when I have read that last chapter."

Read the last chapter of Revelation. How does it inspire you?

In the Bible, oil often represents the presence of the Holy Spirit.

How are you keeping oil in the lamp of your life?

What if you knew Jesus was going to return in your lifetime?

How would it change the way you live?

Write Boldness Into Your Life

5

Have you ever been to a prayer meeting or worship service and saw someone whose prayers and praise seemed to be filled with power and confidence? It isn't the words they say or how they say it. There is something in their demeanor—an assurance, a boldness, as they interact with God.

That was normal in the early church, but in modern times, many Christians have lost the strength in their spiritual lives. David Mains, author of *The Sense of His Presence*, wrote, "I'm convinced that boldness for the most part is lacking in the prayers of the church and desperately needs to be rediscovered."

But how can boldness be "discovered"? Isn't it just a personality trait? Actually, the Bible includes several ways to add confidence to your spiritual life.

First, the early Christians asked God for boldness (Acts 4:29). The Holy Spirit answered their prayer, giving them steadfast confidence even in the midst of Rome's torturous persecution. God answers fervent prayers of believers. Jesus said, "Ask, and it will be given to you; seek, and you will find; knock, and it will be opened to you" (Matthew 7:7).

Second, righteous living will give you boldness. Proverbs 28:1 says, "… The righteous are bold as a lion." This kind of boldness doesn't come from self-righteousness. It is confidence in the righteousness of Christ. Mains explains, "Some might think boldness in prayer means storming into heaven's courts demanding attention. This is not boldness in the way Christ taught it or modeled it. Instead, boldness is the picture of a confident servant coming to his master in an attitude of praise."

This is the same kind of boldness that enabled Esther to entreat her husband, the king, to save her people. This is the same boldness that urged Moses to ask God to see His glory. Biblical boldness comes with humility in our own abilities and confidence in God's, knowing with Him, nothing is impossible.

God gave the early church boldness when they fervently prayed for it.

Write a prayer asking God to give you the kind of boldness that He gave the early church.

Second Corinthians 3:12 says, "Since we have such a hope, we are very bold …"

How do you find boldness in the hope you have in Christ?

Acts 4:13 says, "When [the people] saw the boldness of Peter and John, and perceived that they were uneducated, common men, they were astonished. And they recognized that they had been with Jesus."

How can a Christian use boldness to exemplify Christ?

Joshua told the people, "Have I not commanded you? Be strong and courageous. Do not be frightened, and do not be dismayed, for the Lord your God is with you wherever you go" (Joshua 1:9).

How does Joshua's encouragement inspire you?

The Roman philosopher Cicero once said, "A man of courage is also full of faith."

What can others know about your faith based on your courage?

_____
_____
_____
_____
_____
_____
_____
_____
_____
_____
_____
_____
_____
_____
_____
_____
_____
_____
_____
_____
_____
_____
_____
_____
_____

Shakespeare wrote, "Virtue is bold, and goodness never fearful."

Why do you think Shakespeare described virtue and goodness this way?

What is the boldest action you have ever taken for Christ?

Write about what you remember.

Thomas "Stonewall" Jackson was a lieutenant general in the Civil War whose bravery was unsurpassed. He never appeared to cower, even in the midst of flying bullets, and led troops into battle without flinching. This characteristic earned him the nickname "Stonewall" by his fellow soldiers.

What made Jackson so fearless in war? He once answered that question: "God has fixed the time for my death. I do not concern myself about that, but to be always ready, no matter when it may overtake me. That is the way all men should live, and then all would be equally brave."

Jackson depended on God's sovereign will. He trusted God's Word, which says, "You have decided the length of our lives. You know how many months we will live, and we are not given a minute longer." (Job 14:5 NLT).

In our day, most of our fears aren't based on bullets, but opinions and judgements of others. Our courage doesn't show in the way we ride a horse, but how we stand on God's Word despite the critics.

So how do we find the courage to live a Stonewall Jackson kind of faith? Second Timothy 1:6-7 gives us a clue: "For this reason I remind you to fan into flame the gift of God, which is in you through the laying on of my hands, for God gave us a spirit not of fear but of power and love and self-control." The Holy Spirit is the source of fearlessness, and in order to deepen that confidence we should "fan into flame" our faith. In other words, help it grow. The more you grow in the faith, the more fearless you become.

Most importantly, remember that God's opinion is more important than man's. Paul said, "For am I now seeking the approval of man, or of God? Or am I trying to please man? If I were still trying to please man, I would not be a servant of Christ" (Galatians 1:10). Serving our Lord will offend some. But it's a small price to pay in order to win the spiritual battles of life.

One of the ways you can fan the flames of your faith is to meditate on the word of God.

Choose a passage that represents an area of growth in your life and write about how it inspires you.

Another way to fan the flame of faith is to pray.

Consider ways you can find more time for prayer.

Read Galatians 1:10 again, and consider your daily life.

Write about the ways you please God and the ways you struggle with pleasing man.

Consider Hebrews 13:6: "So we can confidently say, 'The Lord is my helper; I will not fear; what can man do to me?'"

How does scripture inspire you?

First John 4:18 says, "There is no fear in love, but perfect love casts out fear. For fear has to do with punishment, and whoever fears has not been perfected in love."

How do you think love casts out fear?

President Franklin D. Roosevelt said, "The only thing we have to fear is fear itself."

Do you think he was right? Why?

In the book *From Fear to Love,* Ray and Nancy Kane wrote, "When fears arise in all our lives, let us recognize and resist the temptation to numb our feelings by seeking wealth, prestige, power, or beauty."

What have you pursued in your own life to control your fears?

We live in a pick-and-choose society. Facebook and YouTube have created a virtual world in which you alone are the star. If someone disagrees with you, you can personalize the audience, shutting out opposing thought. Amazon customizes resources for you, and then you can choose to tailor your own Christmas gifts by imposing your wish list.

It's no surprise then that people want to customize their spiritual beliefs, too. In *Futurecast*, George Barna wrote, "We are a designer society. We want everything customized to our personal needs—our clothing, our food, our education," He goes on to include religion. "People say, 'I believe in God. I believe the Bible is a good book. And then I believe whatever I want.'"

Those with this mindset are deceived by our cherry-picking society. Instead of seeking truth and changing their lives to accommodate, they insist that truth change to suit the latest fads. They lack discernment, which is the ability to recognize truth from lies. The Apostle Paul described these Christians as "tossed to and fro by the waves and carried about by every wind of doctrine, by human cunning, by craftiness in deceitful schemes" (Ephesians 4:14). They follow the ever-popular advice to "follow your heart." But the heart's longings change with the whims of life.

Jeremiah 17:9 says, "The heart is deceitful above all things, and desperately sick; who can understand it?" We can't trust our feelings to discern the truth. It is too easily swayed.

But Hebrews 4:12 tells us what we can trust. "For the word of God is living and active, sharper than any two-edged sword, piercing to the division of soul and of spirit, of joints and of marrow, and discerning the thoughts and intentions of the heart." Truth has been made clear in the Bible. By reading it, we can learn Christ's teachings and ways and gather wisdom and discernment for life.

Wisdom and discernment go hand in hand. James 1:5 says, "If any of you lacks wisdom, let him ask God, who gives generously to all without reproach, and it will be given him."

Write a prayer asking God for wisdom.

Discernment helps us see the difference between what is truth and what is a lie. First Thessalonians 5:21 tells us to "test everything."

What does this mean for your life?

Proverbs 15:14 says, "The heart of him who has understanding seeks knowledge, but the mouths of fools feed on folly."

Where do you get most of your information about life?
Does it come from scripture or somewhere else?

Thomas a Kempis said, "We must not trust every saying or suggestion, but warily and patiently ponder things according to the will of God."

Write several ways you can confirm the veracity of information according to the Bible.

In a speech given by Walter Kotschnig to a college in 1940, he said, "Don't be so open minded that your brains fall out."

How does this apply to our culture today?

Oswald Chambers wrote, "God does not exist to answer our prayers, but by our prayers we come to discern the mind of God."

What do you think Chambers meant by this?

Charles Spurgeon said, "Discernment is not a matter of simply telling the difference between right and wrong; rather it is telling the difference between right and almost right."

What does Spurgeon mean by this?

Private Desmond Doss volunteered as a medic in World War II, even though he was a pacifist and refused to carry a gun. He was sent to one of the bloodiest war zones—Okinawa, Japan—without a weapon to defend himself. Americans were being slaughtered. When the orders came to retreat, dozens of injured men were trapped at the top of the 30-foot cliff.

With Japanese bullets flying, Doss carried one injured man at a time to the edge of the cliff, lowered him by rope and went after another. After each rescue, exhausted and bleeding from blisters, Doss prayed for strength, "Just one more, Lord. Just one more." He eventually saved around 75 injured men single-handedly, unarmed and unshielded.

There are times in life when circumstances seem insurmountable. It may be sickness, depression, or bills piling high. But we don't have to have enough strength to carry the burden all at once; we just need enough strength to make it through one more day.

Jesus said, "... Do not be anxious about tomorrow, for tomorrow will be anxious for itself. Sufficient for the day is its own trouble" (Matthew 6:34). Just like Doss, we can pray to pay off "just one more bill," or make it through "one more day" of sickness.

The writer of Hebrews encourages Christians to live out their faith like a runner in a race. A runner doesn't flail around wasting energy and time. He doesn't try to finish the race in one leap. But he paces himself, taking each step—one after another—until he finishes and receives the prize (Hebrews 12:1-2).

Jesus told us to share our faith with others. He told us to give generously and be kind to those who mistreat us. Thinking about the task as a whole is overwhelming. All we really have to do is share with just one person; give to just one mission; give grace to just one enemy. And then another. All we need right now is the strength for just one more.

Hebrews 10:36 says, "... You have need of endurance, so that when you have done the will of God you may receive what is promised."

How does endurance help you obtain God's promises?

"Rejoice in hope, be patient in tribulation, be constant in prayer" (Romans 12:12).

How does this advice help you endure the challenges of life?

In Revelation 2:3, Jesus said, "I know you are enduring patiently and bearing up for my name's sake, and you have not grown weary."

How does it help you to know that Jesus sees your patient endurance?

Hebrews 12:7 says, "It is for discipline that you have to endure. God is treating you as sons. For what son is there whom his father does not discipline?"

How does this scripture reassure you?

Hymn writer and clergyman Phillip Brooks said, "Do not pray for easy lives, pray to be stronger men. Do not pray for tasks equal to your powers, pray for powers equal to your tasks."

How does Brooks' quote inspire you?

Henry David Thoreau wrote, "The price of anything is the amount of life you exchange for it."

How important is the endurance of the Gospel to you?

Hellen Keller said, "Although the world is very full of suffering, it is also full of the overcoming of it."

Write about times in your life where you overcame suffering and are better for it.

In 1877, the White House was declared "alcohol free" by First Lady Lucy Hayes, an action that earned her the title "Lemonade Lucy" by her critics. But Mrs. Hayes had the gift of hospitality, and her frequent parties were always popular, even among her wine-drinking critics. Everyone was eager to attend any event hosted by Lucy Hayes, simply because she knew how to throw a good party, and her company was sheer delight. She was known for her compassion, charming demeanor, and steadfast faith.

But Lucy wasn't just a hostess to the aristocracy of 1600 Pennsylvania Avenue. She was also known as "Mother Lucy" by the military. President Rutherford B. Hayes was elected to office in the wake of the Civil War. During the war, his wife was not afraid to step onto battlegrounds to attend the wounded bodies and hearts of the weary soldiers. As her husband fought as a Union general, Lucy followed behind, bringing an occasional word of encouragement, a clean bandage, or a prayer to the troops. As First Lady, she continued her love and care for the military.

The exhortation to be hospitable is found throughout the Old and New Testaments. Hospitality doesn't require an outgoing personality. It doesn't require a lot of money. The gift is more than just the ability to throw a good party. It encompasses caring for strangers, giving to the poor, even offering a drink to a thirsty soul. It just requires a willing heart, one that looks for ways to encourage others.

Acts of hospitality were mentioned by Jesus many times, and He often explained it as a service done to Him personally. In Matthew 25:40, He said, "Truly, I say to you, as you did it to one of the least of these my brothers, you did it to me." May we see the face of Jesus in every stranger, every visitor, and every friend we meet.

Who do you know that could benefit from some hospitality?

What can you do to bless them?

Hospitality doesn't have to be costly.

Make a list of hospitality ideas that cost little to no money.

Hebrew 13:2 says, "Do not neglect to show hospitality to strangers, for thereby some have entertained angles unawares."

How does this challenge and inspire you?

Like the case with Lucy Hayes, sometimes the best intentions still draw criticism, but it's important to remember that "such sacrifices are pleasing to God." (Hebrews 13:16).

How can you graciously continue to serve even in the face of mockery?

God sees your service to the least, and He will reward you. Jesus said, "…
When you give a feast, invite the poor, the crippled, the lame, the blind, and
you will be blessed, because they cannot repay you. For you will be repaid at
the resurrection of the just" (Luke 14:13-14).

How does this encourage and challenge you?

In the book *The personal Touch*, Rachael Crabb and Raeann Hart wrote, "The emphasis in our practice of hospitality should be on how we give of ourselves to minster to others—not on how we perform to entertain others."

What does this mean to you?

In her book *Everyday Hospitality*, Thea Jarvis writes, "Ideally, hospitality is the outward expression of an inner attitude, a virtue that erupts from the heart, spilling out toward others."

How can you live out this kind of hospitality in your life?

Pastor Rick Warren once said, "Humility is not thinking less about yourself. It's thinking about yourself less." Many Christians believe humility means identifying only personal imperfections and rejecting compliments. Ironically, that actually keeps the focus on self, just from a negative perspective. True humility takes the spotlight off our thoughts and feelings and focuses on God's will and ministering to others.

In addition, are made in the image of God, so it can be hard to remember we are not God. As the song "Big Enough" by Chris Rice says, "… The mirror's another place where we wrestle face to face with the image of deity." While every human has importance as God's image bearers, we can't forget that the only reason we are important is because of Him.

So how can we be both important and humble? The Apostle Paul describes humility this way: "Do nothing from selfish ambition or conceit, but in humility count others more significant than yourselves. Let each of you look not only to his own interests, but also to the interests of others. Have this mind among yourselves, which is yours in Christ Jesus, who, though he was in the form of God, did not count equality with God a thing to be grasped, but emptied himself, by taking the form of a servant …" (Philippians 2:3-7).

This passage offers several paths for humility: *First*, we are exhorted to regard ourselves as servants to others. Consider, how can you be a servant wife? Coworker? Church member?

Second, look at circumstances from another's viewpoint. This even applies to the person who is always offended or always right. This is true for the person who hyper-focuses on offending others and never apologizes. One point of view is not all that matters.

Third, humility doesn't take score. It doesn't grumble, "That's not fair." Humility doesn't nurture egos and measure what we "deserve."

Does that mean you have to endure a life of being run over? No! James 4:10 says, "Humble yourselves before the Lord, and he will exalt you." Like Jesus was exalted because of His humility, we will also be rewarded in the life to come.

Write down any struggles you have with pride and humility.

What are some ways you can work on those areas of struggle?

Think of someone you know that exemplifies humility.

What qualities do you see? How can you emulate those?

English minister Obadiah Grew said, "By humility, I do not mean the abjectness of a base mind; but a prudent care not to over-value ourselves upon any account."

What does this mean for your life?

Samuel Rutherford said, "Humility is a strange flower; it grows best in winter weather, and under storms of affliction."

Why do you think this was Rutherford's description?

Scottish minister and scholar Robert Leighton said, "God's choice acquaintances are humble men." Look up "humble" in your Bible concordance and consider those who are described in the scripture this way.

What characteristics do you think makes these people "humble"?

James 4:6 says, "God opposes the proud but gives grace to the humble."

How does this scripture challenge you?

Proverbs 22:4 says, "The reward for humility and fear of the Lord is riches and honor and life."

What are some ways you have seen this truth principle in your life?
What are some ways you may see it in the future?

_____

_____

_____

_____

_____

_____

_____

_____

_____

_____

_____

_____

_____

_____

_____

_____

_____

_____

_____

_____

_____

_____

_____

_____

"I have prayed and asked God to give me peace, but it's like He doesn't hear me," Julie said. The death of her daughter made her reflect back to her childhood faith. So she sought council with her Christian friend, Marie.

Marie asked, "Have you found a church?" Julie said she went a couple times, but nothing permanent.

"Where are you in your Bible reading?" Marie went on. Julie admitted she read a couple of scriptures on the Internet, but she hadn't actually opened the Bible.

"I just want God to answer my prayers," Julie said. "Why doesn't God just do what I ask Him to do?"

Marie replied lovingly, "Honestly, Julie, He probably wonders the same thing about you."

You see, Julie already knew from her childhood faith that she should go to church. She knew she should read the Bible. But Julie wanted God's intervention without obedience.

People in Jesus' day had the same misunderstanding, and He asked them, "Why do you call me 'Lord, Lord' and not do what I tell you?" (Luke 6:46). Like Julie, we so often ask God to intervene in our lives, but we don't want to do what He has already commanded us to do—like pray, attend fellowship with other Christians, receive teaching, and read the Bible. If we did, we would already have many answers. They may not always be the answers we like, but there would be some peace, despite the present circumstances.

Jesus went on to explain this to the crowd: "Everyone who comes to me and hears my words [which are found in the Bible] and does them, I will show you what he is like: he is like a man building a house, who dug deep and laid the foundation on the rock. And when a flood arose, the stream broke against that house and could not shake it, because it had been well built" (Luke 6:47-48).

If you want the kind of life that withstands the strongest storms and the kind of relationship with God that provides the benefits of peace and hope, test your faithful obedience to God's Word.

Dietrich Bonhoeffer said, "Only he who believes is obedient. Only he who is obedient believes."

How does this statement inspire and challenge you?

Evan Henry Hopkins, author of *Thoughts on Life and Godliness*, wrote, "Ask yourself, does my heavenly Father set before me a path of obedience along which the Spirit and power of Christ cannot lead me?"

How would you answer this question?

Andrew Murray wrote, "The blessedness and the blessing of God's word is only to be known by doing it."

How does this challenge and inspire you?

In John 14:15, Jesus said, "If you love me, you will keep my commandments."

What does your obedience say about your love for Christ?
What does your disobedience say?

The Psalmist said, "I have chosen the way of faithfulness; I set your rules before me." (Psalm 119:30).

How can you apply the same principle to your life?

Which commandments do you struggle to obey?

What can you do to improve?

Think back to a time when you obeyed God, despite pressure not to.

How did you benefit? What did you learn from that experience?

What do you think of when you hear the word *sacrifice?* Maybe you think of a lamb or goat. Maybe you think of raising kids or another selfless, loving act. Maybe you think of something someone gave up for you. Sacrifice is often associated with love. But have you ever associated sacrifice with *hope?*

Sacrifice doesn't just affect the here and now. It changes the future. Most sacrifice is an investment. It says "no" to something now for something better later.

Paul exhorts us, "I appeal to you therefore, brothers, by the mercies of God, to present your bodies as a living sacrifice, holy and acceptable to God, which is your spiritual worship" (Romans 12:1). As Christians, we no longer need sacrifices of dead animals. Jesus was the final lamb. Now, we offer ourselves as a living sacrifice. But how?

First, offer a sacrifice of praise (Hebrews 13:15). This means giving praise, even when we don't feel like it. This doesn't mean our praise is inauthentic or fake. It's a praise of hope in *God's* answered promises to come! We may not have the answers yet, but we praise God for what we know He will *do* in the future.

Second, don't neglect doing good and sharing out of your abundance (Hebrews 13:16). The Bible tells us to give sacrificially and cheerfully. This includes tithing. According to several studies, on average, only 10 to 25 percent of the congregation gives to the church. Giving to your local church is the best way to reach hurting people who need help in your hometown and around the world. Your sacrifice now creates hope for someone else's future.

Third, sacrifice your time. Jesus called us to be servants like Him. He loved, cared, and took the time to talk to the hurting, outcast, and despairing. How Jesus lived was "a fragrant offering and sacrifice to God." (Ephesians 5:2). And we are called to be like Him.

Invest in your faith, in the faith of others, and invest in the gospel. Offer yourself as a living sacrifice and see the blessings of God in your future.

What are some practical specific ways you can sacrifice for others?

Where can you give of your money? Your time? Your thoughts?

Consider times when you have sacrificed something now for a better future.

What did you lose? What did you gain?

Think of times when someone sacrificed for your sake.

What did they lose? What did you gain?

G. K. Chesterton said, "A man should not sacrifice what he does not esteem." In other words, a sacrifice is not really a sacrifice if it causes no pain.

How does this thought challenge you?

Elisabeth Elliot understood sacrifice. After her husband was killed by an indigenous people group, she continued to serve and minister to the people for many years. She said, "I will offer [God] both my tears and my exultation. Nothing we offer Him will be lost."

How does her example speak to you?

Hebrews 13:15 says, "Through him then let us continually offer up a sacrifice of praise to God, that is, the fruit of lips that acknowledge his name."

How would you describe a "sacrifice of praise"?
How can you offer such a sacrifice?

Ephesians 5:1-2 says, "Therefore be imitators of God, as beloved children. And walk in love, as Christ loved us and gave himself up for us, a fragrant offering and sacrifice to God."

How can you follow Christ's example in this way?

Nehemiah was a righteous man. He loved God's law, and he loved Jerusalem. As a young man, Nehemiah vowed to rebuild the walls that had fallen around Jerusalem, and that's exactly what he did. When they were finished, he dedicated the walls by reading God's law. It had been many years since the people had heard God's law, and they began weeping in shame. Guilt filled their hearts because of their sins. But Nehemiah stopped them. He told them to celebrate, not mourn. Get out the best wine and food. Because, "… The joy of the Lord is your strength" (Nehemiah 8:10).

You see, there is no strength in mourning our sins or playing the victim. Awareness of sin is good, but only because it demonstrates the grace and mercy of God. Jesus came to give us "a beautiful headdress instead of ashes, the oil of gladness instead of mourning, the garment of praise instead of a faint spirit; that [we] may be called oaks of righteousness" (Isaiah 61:3). Through His grace, we have the strength of joy.

Strength is found in strange places. Joy is only one secret path to strength. Another is found in Isaiah 40:31, which says those who wait on God will renew their strength. We don't have to panic or get ahead of His timing. Again, the root of strength is trusting God's character, not our own. That confidence allows us to stand on God's Word when logic and anxiety tempt us to take circumstances into our own hands.

Finally, we can find strength in our imperfections. When the Apostle Paul asked God to take away a troubling issue in his life, God said, "My grace is sufficient for you, for my power is made perfect in weakness." And Paul responded by concluding to boast in his weaknesses. "For when I am weak," he said, "then I am strong" (2 Corinthians 12:9-10).

Strength isn't easily found. All three of these—joy through mourning, waiting, and imperfections—are unlikely treasure chests. But open them in your life and see how strong you will be.

Every weakness has a strength.

What are your weaknesses, and how can God use them to do His will?

What is causing anxiety and/or worry in your life right now? How can you let go of control and trust God?

Read Matthew 6:25-35. How does this passage speak to you?

What did Nehemiah mean by "the joy of the Lord is our strength?"

How can you find strength in joy?

When you find yourself waiting on God, what can you do in order to sustain yourself spiritually?

How is waiting valuable?

Andrew Murray wrote, "Since God Himself is a steadfast Rock, the foundation of all certitude and steadfastness, it must be by faith or holding fast to God that man can become steadfast."

How does faith in God make you stronger?

First Corinthians 10:13 says, "No temptation has overtaken you that is not common to man. God is faithful, and he will not let you be tempted beyond your ability, but with the temptation he will also provide the way of escape, that you may be able to endure it."

In what ways has God provided escapes for you in the past?
What escape is He providing for you now?

Deuteronomy 20:4 describes God as "he who goes with you to fight for you against your enemies, to give you the victory."

How does this comfort you?

Caleb and Kate enjoyed studying together. Kate was a dedicated Christian, and Caleb was agnostic, but things soon got romantic between them. One day, studying turned into kissing, and Caleb was pressing to go further.

"I'm not going to have sex with you," Kate said. "I'm a Christian, and I plan to stay a virgin until I get married."

"That's the problem with you Christians," Caleb said. "You don't want to have any fun."

"You think that's the reason?" Kate laughed. "God gives us rules not to keep us from having fun, but to protect us. If I have sex with you, I could get a disease, or I could get pregnant. At the very least, I would get emotionally attached in a relationship that may not last. Sex makes a bond that cannot be broken."

"Wow," Caleb said, stunned. "No one has ever told me anything like that before."

Living righteously isn't just for hyper-religious or self-righteous people. Righteousness just means living in the way God tells us to live—the best way—for our good and the good of others. God set boundaries to protect us and help us grow and to provide a path to our truest joy and peace.

These rules and boundaries don't take away freedom; they actually give us more. Think of a school on a hill that has no fence around the yard. The children stay far away from the road, huddled close together toward the school. Teachers must be hyper-diligent to keep the children from getting into the street or leaving the property. But if the school yard has a fence, the children can go all over the yard freely. They can play with balls and not fear them rolling into traffic. Teachers can be more relaxed. The boundary actually gives everyone more room, less anxiety, and more protection.

That's what righteous living does for God's people. When we live within the bounds of God's rules, we actually have more freedom to enjoy all the things God has in store for us in this life.

Read the Ten Commandments in Exodus 20:1-17.

How do each of these rules actually give God's people more freedom?

Think of the rules your parents, grandparents, or teachers made you follow as a child.

How were their rules good for you?

Consider the rules and boundaries in your own life.

Would you describe your life as righteous? How would others describe it?

John Maxwell, author of *Be All You Can Be* wrote, "It is when we live by the right principles that we begin to love the right principles. Most of the time, we want to fall in love with what is right and then have it happen to us."

Do you agree or disagree? Why?

In *The Shepherd Psalm*, F. B. Meyer wrote, "Christ's leadings are always along 'paths of righteousness.'"

How does this idea challenge you?

Psalm 106:3 says, "Blessed are they who observe justice, who do righteousness at all times!"

How have you seen this truth in your life and others'?

First Peter 3:14 says, "...Even if you should suffer for righteousness' sake, you will be blessed. Have no fear of [your adversaries], nor be troubled..."

How does this verse comfort you?

Chris struggled with homosexual thoughts as a single man, but because he was a Christian, he celebrated the day he overcame his struggle and married a woman. Jennifer and Amanda were friends with Chris. Amanda supported Chris, but Jennifer was concerned. She asked Amanda, "Why do you think this is good? Why should Chris deny his feelings and suppress them to be someone he's not?"

Amanda replied, "Jennifer, let me put it this way. When you see Chris, you see a man who was free now walking into a cage. When I see Chris, I see a man who was bound in a cage, and now he's been set free."

Paul told us, "For freedom Christ has set us free" (Galatians 5:1). That freedom doesn't mean we won't struggle with problems and sinful desires. We still have a flesh with all its corrupt cravings. But the spirit of every believer is pure, and it is free from the tyranny of feelings, temptations, and lusts. The Holy Spirit has the power to overcome every evil thought (2 Corinthians 10:5).

We are also free from the fear of God's wrath. There is no longer punishment for those who trust in Christ. Their sins are not counted against them. Some may take that as permission to sin. If there is no punishment, what keeps us from indulging any sin we want? Why not party, steal, and take advantage of others? The answer is that a reformed spirit no longer desires darkness. As we grow, we discover the harm of sin and the value of righteousness.

First Corinthians 6:12 sums it up, "'All things are lawful for me,' but not all things are helpful. 'All things are lawful for me,' but I will not be dominated by anything." Whatever controls your actions, is also what enslaves you.

Let us not be slaves to sin, but free servants of Christ. All we do for Christ is to be done out of love, not obligation. As English theologian Thomas Goodwin said, "Grace is the freeness of love." When love manifests itself fully, the result is not captivity, but freedom.

Have you ever felt bound up by the Christian life? Why or why not?

What does this reveal about yourself?

Name some of the things Christ set you free from.

How did you change?

John Milton wrote, "None can love freedom heartily but good men; the rest love not freedom but license."

What does Milton mean by this?

In her book *For Women Only*, Gigi Graham Tchividjian wrote, "When God gave us the gift of freedom, He placed it within a framework. He also gave us a well-defined guideline for the effective use of this gift."

How do God's guidelines empower you to do what He called you to do?

Jay Adams said, "Freedom in God's world never comes apart from structure."

How does this quote challenge and inspire you?

Second Corinthians 3:17 says, "Now the Lord is the Spirit, and where the Spirit of the Lord is, there is freedom."

How does this scripture apply to your life?

First Peter 2:16 says, "Live as people who are free, not using your freedom as a cover-up for evil, but living as servants of God."

How can your freedom pave the way for serving God?

Author Thomas Haliburton wrote, "Women will sometimes confess their sins, but I never knew one to confess her *faults.*"

Why is it so hard for us to admit when we are wrong? Saying, "I'm sorry" is not so hard. What's hard is leaving off the "but …" in order to justify our behavior.

Children do this all the time. Suzie does something annoying to Johnny. Johnny pushes Suzie. Suzie tells on Johnny, and Johnny tells on Suzie. Instead of admitting fault and accepting apologies, the children tell a parent who can punish the other child. Young and old, we all want justice—a moral reckoning. Paul said, "They [mankind] show that the work of the law [God's standard] is written on their hearts, while their conscience also bears witness, and their conflicting thoughts accuse or even excuse them" (Romans 2:15).

Paul explains how men naturally want to prove guilt or innocence. And yet, we are all guilty before God. Romans 3:10 says, "None is righteous, no, not one." The pursuit of justification is a losing battle. It only brings division and sorrow.

But confession offers joy and peace to the soul. It's as important to your life as a plumbing system is to a skyscraper. There has to be a way to dispose of the refuse, or else it overflows and desecrates. John told us, "If we confess our sins, [God] is faithful and just to forgive us our sins and to cleanse us from all unrighteousness" (1 John 1:9). And James implored, "Confess your sins to one another and pray for one another, that you may be healed" (James 5:16).

Confession is not easy. It requires humility and grace through the power of the Holy Spirit. The next time you have the opportunity to confess, look for the all-too-familiar "but" and resist the temptation to use it. As a result, you will find peace. Even if the one you offended continues to hold a grudge, know that in God's eyes, your confession was holy and He has forgiven you.

Think about the last time you prayed about specific sins and asked God to forgive you.

What was the effect on your life?

Take the time to confess any struggles with specific sins.

Write about your experience.

D. L. Moody once said, "Let your confession be as wide as your transgression."

How does this challenge you?

Clement was a leader in the early church. He wrote to the Corinthians, "The Lord, brethren, stands in need of nothing; and He desires nothing of anyone, except that confession be made to Him."

How does this inspire and challenge you?

Proverbs 28:13 says, "Whoever conceals his transgressions will not prosper, but he who confesses and forsakes them will obtain mercy."

Why do you think Solomon said this?

There is always something to confess. First John 1:8 says, "If we say we have no sin, we deceive ourselves, and the truth is not in us."

Should you confess every day? Why or why not?

God will not turn you away, no matter what you've done. James 4:8 says, "Draw near to God, and he will draw near to you. Cleanse your hands, you sinners, and purify your hearts …"

How does this comfort you?

Sex is a magnificent connection that can feel like magic. God created it to be enjoyed by a man and his wife and to fulfill His command to "be fruitful and multiply." When sex takes place within God's boundaries, it is beautiful.

But the current culture has taken sex out of its sacred space and perverted it. Now, it's a measure of status, a form of currency, an experience to define and dictate life. People define who they are by sexual performance, instead of character and integrity. Pornography is a $97 billion industry. That's more money than Major League Baseball, the NFL, and the NBA combined. Human trafficking has claimed 40.3 million victims, and 25 percent of them are children. Movies, television, and commercials normalize deviant behavior and even celebrate it.

While everyone goes on as if there is no harm, no foul, millions of victims are left in the wake. Children are abused, tortured, and murdered. Marriages suffer. It's becoming normal to use porn as a sexual tool for couples. But Jesus said, "… Everyone who looks at a woman [other than his wife] with lustful intent has already committed adultery with her in his heart" (Matthew 5:28). Porn is an affair of the heart, and it comes at a cost. Reports show that excessive porn use can make men even in their 20s impotent. And porn addiction can lead to acting out fantasies in real life.

You may not think your home or church has been affected, but if you have the internet, YouTube, smart phones, Netflix, or cable, you have an open door for the sexual "revolution" to march in.

The Psalmist wrote, "How can a young man keep his way pure? By guarding it according to your word" (Psalm 119:9). The word of God has the power to break the obsession with perverted sex. The Holy Spirit gives us the power to "destroy arguments and every lofty opinion raised against the knowledge of God, and take every thought captive to obey Christ" (2 Corinthians 10:5). It's time to take this enemy seriously and start fighting for purity.

Romans 12:2 says, "Do not be conformed to this world, but be transformed by the renewal of your mind, that by testing you may discern what is the will of God, what is good and acceptable and perfect."

Write a prayer asking God to keep your mind renewed.

What are some practical ways you can protect your mind, your family, and your home from media and other types of impure content?

Make a list of some practical ideas.

How has your sexuality shaped your life?

How does your identity in Christ change the way you see sexuality?

Joshua Harris wrote, "A relationship devoid of purity is soon reduced to nothing more than two bodies grasping at and demanding pleasure."

Do you agree or disagree? Why?

Blaise Pascal said, "The stream is always purer at its source."

How can you stay closer to our source, Jesus Christ?

First Corinthians 6:18 says, "Flee from sexual immorality. Every other sin a person commits is outside the body, but the sexually immoral person sins against his own body."

How can you flee sexual immorality in your own life?

Pray this prayer from Psalm 51:10, "Create in me a clean heart, O God, and renew a right spirit within me."

Write what you hear God say to your heart.

Write Zealousness Into Your Life

18

In his book *A Plea for Zeal*, Samuel Ward described Christian zeal as "a spiritual heat wrought in the heart of man by the Holy Ghost, improving the good affections of love, joy, etc., for the furtherance of God's glory, His word, His house, His saints, and salvation of souls."

Fire has been used throughout history to cleanse, purify, create, and give light. Life wouldn't be possible without it. Ward describes zeal the same way for believers. A Christian without zeal is like a person without fire—spiritually lifeless. Hebrews 12:29 says, "For our God is a consuming fire." The Holy Spirit literally fills us with the spiritual fire of God's nature.

Many tend to see zeal as the opposite of Christian virtues, favoring nonconfrontational and tender characteristics over ones that could be taken as reckless or extreme. But Jesus told us to "love the Lord your God with all your heart and with all your soul and with all your mind and with all your *strength*" (Mark 12:30, emphasis added). He told the church at Laodicea their faith was lukewarm, and He warned them to "be zealous and repent" lest He spew them from His mouth (Revelation 3:16). Even Jesus was zealous. He overturned tables and drove money-changers out of the temple with a whip. John described Him by the prophecy of Psalm 69:9: "Zeal for your house will consume me" (John 2:13-17).

Zeal characterizes the subjects and objects we love. Think about the topics you can't wait to talk about: clearance sales at your favorite store, your child's great accomplishment, trips to exotic locations. The zeal of those topics should pale in comparison to your zeal of sharing the gospel.

Of course, like any virtue, zealousness can be used inappropriately, like the time Peter cut off the ear of the soldier who tried to take Jesus away. But even Peter's misplaced passion could not ruin God's perfect plan. Jesus healed the Roman's ear with a touch. Don't let fear of passion take away your passion. God can handle it.

In Psalm 122:1, David wrote, "I was glad when they said to me, 'Let us go to the house of the Lord!'" When was the last time you felt excited to go to church? Or have your Sunday mornings become dreaded and routine?

Write a prayer asking God to restore your zeal for His gathering place.

Romans 12:11 says, "Do not be slothful in zeal, be fervent in spirit, serve the Lord."

Do these words describe your faith? Why or why not?

Ecclesiastes 9:10 says, "Whatever your hands find to do, do it with your might …"

How can you apply this to your walk of faith?

Think of a person you would describe as "zealous."

What qualities do you see? What qualities do you want to emulate?

What topics are you are zealous about: Hobbies, movies, music, fashion, sports, television shows, food, apps, relationships?

What makes you zealous about those things?

Ancient church historian Thomas Fuller wrote, "Zeal is fit only for wise men, but is found mostly in fools."

What do you think Fuller meant by this?"

William James, author of *The Varieties of Religious Experience: A Study in Human Nature* described passion as, "the habitual center of [one's] personal energy."

What does your passion say about you?
How does this pertain to your spiritual life?

_____
_____
_____
_____
_____
_____
_____
_____
_____
_____
_____
_____
_____
_____
_____
_____
_____
_____
_____
_____
_____
_____
_____
_____
_____

Becca tried to explain to Suzanne what a relationship with God is like. "You know how it felt to be a little girl, sitting in your father's lap?" Becca asked. "A relationship with God is like the moment daddy wraps his arms around you, and you know everything is going to be alright."

"That makes no sense to me," Suzanne responded. "My father left when I was a child, and I never had that kind of relationship with him."

Families are meant to be a reflection of God's love for His people (see Ephesians 5). Unfortunately, many of us grew up without the unconditional love of a father, and it handicaps our view of God. Rampant divorce, abandonment, and abuse have tainted the idea of "father," so a Father in heaven sounds trite, even dreadful.

But the Bible encourages us to have childlike faith. How is that possible if the image of God as Father has been tainted? How is that possible if your childhood was filled with survival, instead of safety, or fear, instead of a firm foundation?

The answer is found in Romans 10:17: "Faith comes from hearing and hearing through the word of Christ." Childlike faith doesn't mean we have a shallow or blind faith. Paul actually cautions us *not* to remain shallow. He said, "When I was a child, I spoke like a child, I thought like a child, I reasoned like a child. When I became a man, I gave up childish ways" (1 Corinthians 13:11).

Childlike faith means we read God's promises and watch Him fulfill what He said He would do. What makes faith childlike is its simplicity, not its naivety. It's a faith that depends on Scripture for growth. Peter reiterates this, saying, "Like newborn infants, long for the pure spiritual milk, that by it you may grow up into salvation" (1 Peter 2:2).

No matter what your earthly father was like, God has a proven record. He loves you unconditionally; He keeps His word perfectly; and He is all you need in this life to really live. Test Him and see.

Jesus said, "Truly, I say to you, unless you turn and become like children, you will never enter the kingdom of heaven. Whoever humbles himself like this child is the greatest in the kingdom of heaven" (Matthew 18:3-4).

What do you think Jesus meant?

What was your childhood relationship with your father like? How does it shape your view of God?

How are the two persons different? How are they similar?

Peter tells us, "Like newborn infants, long for the pure spiritual milk, that by it you may grow up into salvation" (1 Peter 2:2).

How does this scripture challenge and inspire you?

Romans 8:14 says, "For all who are led by the Spirit of God are sons [and daughters] of God."

What does it mean to be a child of God? How does this affect your faith?

In her book *Whole Language: Theory in Use*, Judith Newman wrote, "Children do not extract meaning from what they hear others saying; they try instead, to relate what has been said to what is going on."

How can this apply to your faith walk?

Have you used "childlike faith" as an excuse to stop growing in your faith?

How does Paul's explanation of "putting away childish things" challenge you?

St. Teresa of Lisieux said, "We must not be discouraged by our faults, for children fall frequently."

How does this comfort and inspire you?

It is doubtful whether anyone enjoys grief. It isn't pleasant, but it is valuable. As William Secker wrote, "… Sorrow is profitable, but unpleasant. As waters are purest when they are in motion, so saints are generally holiest when in affliction."

Grief reminds us that life isn't the way it should be. Evil exists; bad guys sometimes win; not all stories have a happy ending. From the moment Adam and Eve rebelled against their Maker, mankind and the whole world were cursed. (Genesis 3:17). Before, earth was a paradise without death, without pain. Now, even those who love and know God cannot see His face. We aren't holy enough. And we long for the day "creation itself will be set free from its bondage to corruption and obtain the freedom of the glory of the children of God" (Romans 8:21).

Grief is fitting for a Christian because it does more than make us sorrowful for our darkened world. By remembering what we lost, we also remember what we've gained. We lost God's perfect order because of our own sin, not just Adam's. We had a part in the chaos and the hurt, and we suffer the consequences. Just as David said when he killed another man to take his wife. "Against you, you only, have I sinned and done what is evil in your sight …" (Psalm 51:4).

Our consequences lead us to remember what we gained. By contemplating the pain and imperfection, we are joyfully filled with hope that Christ makes all things new (Revelation 21:5). The effects of sin may alter our lives, but Christ has overcome sin and death. With the Holy Spirit living in us, we can experience peace and joy despite our circumstances.

Even though grief requires us to focus on the losses of sin, it opens the door to praise for our gains. As Solomon said, there is "a time to weep, and a time to laugh; a time to mourn, and a time to dance" (Ecclesiastes 3:4). We can strengthen the positive opposite with the sorrow of the negative.

Psalms 34:18 says, "The Lord is near to the brokenhearted and saves the crusted in spirit."

Why do you think God is near to the brokenhearted?
How does this comfort you?

Jesus said, "Blessed are those who mourn, for they shall be comforted" (Matthew 5:4).

How can those who mourn be blessed? Make a list of possibilities.

John 11:35 tells us, "Jesus wept."

What does it mean to you that Jesus felt sorrow?

Consider a time in your life when you faced great distress or grief.

What were the valuable lessons and character traits you gained?

Psalm 56:8 tells us that God keeps our tears in a bottle.

How is this thought comforting to you?

William Cowper said, "Greif is itself a medicine."

How does this inspire and challenge you?

The playwriter Oscar Wilde said, "Where there is sorrow there is holy ground."

What do you think Wilde meant by this?

Write Mercy Into Your Life

21

A friend attempted to console the dying Thomas Hooker, Christian minister and cofounder of Connecticut. He said, "Sir, you are going to receive the reward of your labour." Hooker replied, "Brother, I am going to receive mercy."

Mercy is God's *refrain* from giving us the punishment we rightly deserve, not to be confused with grace. Grace is the *offer* of God's good gifts we did not earn. Hooker was expressing his astonishment that God would allow him into Heaven, which is a place reserved only for the holy.

Throughout history, God's wrath burned against the sins of mankind, but He often held back His wrath to show mercy. Peter said, "The Lord is not slow to fulfill his promise as some count slowness, but is patient toward you, not wishing that any should perish, but that all should reach repentance" (2 Peter 3:9). God's patience is for the sake of mercy.

God calls us to follow in His steps of mercy. Jesus said, "Be merciful, even as your Father is merciful" (Luke 6:36). We should never find excitement in giving people "what they deserve." Even when punishment or discipline is inevitable, we should administer the pain with grief in our hearts, not sadistic enjoyment. Jesus said, "Blessed are the merciful, for they shall receive mercy" (Matthew 5:7). Living by the virtue of mercy will bring mercy upon your own life when you need it.

We so often want to live by the Old Testament law, "an eye for an eye and a tooth for a tooth," and seek revenge. But Jesus said, "If anyone slaps you on the right cheek, turn to him the other also" (Matthew 5:39).

Does this mean justice will never be done? No. Paul said, "Beloved, never avenge yourselves, but leave it to the wrath of God, for it is written, 'Vengeance is mine, I will repay, says the Lord'" (Romans 12:19). When we choose the path of mercy and leave the justice to God, we live a life of reward.

James 2:13 says, "… Judgment is without mercy to one who has shown no mercy. Mercy triumphs over judgment."

How does this scripture challenge you and inspire you?

Jesus tells us to be merciful like the Father is merciful (Luke 6:36).

What are some ways you can live out this command of Christ?

Write a prayer asking God to give you a heart of mercy.

If there is someone on your mind, pray for that person specifically.

Write about a time when someone showed you mercy.

What happened and how did God's mercy change you?

Tim Keller said, "Mercy and forgiveness must be free and unmerited to the wrongdoer. If the wrongdoer has to do something to merit it, then it isn't mercy."

How does this quote challenge you?

Charles Spurgeon said, "The Lord's mercy often rides to the door of our heart upon the black horse of affliction."

What is the "black horse of affliction"? How has it brought mercy into your life?

Hebrews 4:16 says, "Let us then with confidence draw near to the throne of grace, that we may receive mercy and find grace to help in time of need."

Draw near to God right now. Talk to Him through writing.

_____

_____

_____

_____

_____

_____

_____

_____

_____

_____

_____

_____

_____

_____

_____

_____

_____

_____

_____

_____

_____

_____

_____

_____

_____

_____

_____

Puritan preacher John Owen said, "For the most part we live upon successes, not promises—unless we see and feel the print of victories, we will not believe." Owen is describing the refusal of some Christians to live with the assurance of hope, the belief that God will do what He says He will do.

The word "hope" has been hijacked by our language to be a synonym of "wish." But "hope" in the biblical sense is more closely related to the words "assurance" and "trust." We don't hope *that* God will do something. We hope *in* God to do something. As Princess Leia said in *Star Wars*, "Help me, Obi-Wan Kenobi. You're my only hope." She didn't mean he was a wish. She meant he was the only way of salvation she had.

Hope is not always easy. It requires waiting on God's timing, not our own. It requires fighting the battle of your mind—the doubts and fears. Hope requires patience. But it finds strength by relying on God's untarnished reputation. He has kept all His promises. And everything He does is for our good, as the often-quoted Jeremiah 29:11 reminds us, "For I know the plans I have for you, declares the Lord, plans for welfare and not for evil, to give you a future and a hope."

So many Christians talk about their sorrows and troubles in an attitude of despair, only *wishing* that God would help them. Instead, let us speak of our pains with hopeful expectation. Paul said, ". . . you may not grieve as others do who have no hope" (1 Thessalonians 4:13).

Hope can be difficult. When everything seems to be going the wrong way, hope says God is going to turn everything around. It takes believing in miracles. But that's the kind of God we serve. He makes the lame walk, the blind see, and the dead live again. There is no greater One in whom to place our hope.

Political mind Jim Wallis wrote, "Hope unbelieved is always considered nonsense. But hope believed is history in the process of being changed."

How can this quote apply to the spiritual life?

George MacDonald said, "To be trusted is a greater compliment than to be love."

What do you think this means?
How does it relate to your relationship with God?

Ralph Waldo Emerson wrote, "All I have seen teaches me to trust the creator for all I have not seen."

How do these words challenge and inspire you?

How has your idea of hope changed throughout these readings?

How will it affect your spiritual life?

When you look at the future, in what or whom do you place your trust?

How does your hope in God compare with everything else?

Hebrews 11:1 says, "Now faith is the assurance of things hoped for, the conviction of things not seen."

Consider how this verse connects hope and faith.

Romans 5:5 says, "And hope does not put us to shame, because God's love has been poured into our hearts through the Holy Spirit who has been given to us."

How does this scripture inspire you?

Hurricane Michael was the worst hurricane to ever hit the Florida panhandle. It caused more than 40 deaths and more than $25 billion in damage. Stephanie Porviliatis and her three children were among those who suffered loss. "There are so many levels to this destruction that no one could have predicted," she wrote, "and I feel completely out of control lately. I'm constantly scared, more anxious than I was before … depressed and worried. Pease tell me I'm not alone."

Stephanie was part of an actual storm that ravaged her life. But there are proverbial storms attacking daily—a life-threatening diagnosis, sudden death of a loved one, the shocking announcement, "I want a divorce." Like Stephanie, we can feel out of control, scared, and alone.

We can't stop the inevitable terrors of life. Jesus actually warned us to expect trials, but He gave us hope. "I have said these things to you, that in me you may have peace. In the world you will have tribulation. But take heart; I have overcome the world" (John 16:33).

When everything in your life feels like it is falling to pieces, there is only one place to find security—in Jesus' presence. He gives meaning to the affliction and a place to belong, even when you feel rejected by everyone else. He gives you a foundation on which to build a new life. Jesus said, "Everyone who hears these words of mine and does them will be like a wise man who built his house on the rock. And the rain fell, and the floods came, and the winds blew and beat on that house, but it did not fall, because it had been founded on the rock" (Matthew 7:24-25).

Notice that Jesus said, "Everyone who hears my words and does them …" Having security in your life is two-fold. First, hear His words, and second, obey them. When you are vulnerable, that's the hardest time to obey Scripture. But remember, God is pleased with your offering, no matter how small. When you walk by faith through the storms of your life, you will find yourself firmly on the rock.

Saint Thomas Aquinas wrote, "If the highest aim of the captain were to preserve his ship, he would keep it in port forever."

How does this quote challenge where you place your security?

Henry Ward Beecher wrote, "The strength of a man consists in finding out the way in which God is going, and going that way too."

Think of examples in your life that support Beecher's statement.

Ernest Hemmingway wrote in *A Farewell to Arms*, "The world breaks everyone, and afterwards many are strong at the broken places."

How does this statement inspire you?

_____

_____

_____

_____

_____

_____

_____

_____

_____

_____

_____

_____

_____

_____

_____

_____

_____

_____

_____

_____

_____

_____

_____

_____

_____

Psalm 18:2 says, "The Lord is my rock and my fortress and my deliverer, my God, my rock, in whom I take refuge, my shield, and the horn of my salvation, my stronghold."

How does this description of God bring stability to your life?

Ephesians 2:19 describes Jesus as the cornerstone of our faith. The cornerstone is the most important part of a structure. It bears the weight of the entire building.

How is Christ the cornerstone of your faith?

What is the hardest part of trusting God for you?

Why do you think that's the case? How can that change?

First Corinthians 3:11 says, "… No one can lay a foundation other than that which is laid, which is Jesus Christ."

How does this scripture build security into your life?

Michelangelo believed God gifted him to tell the story of heaven through art. For him, art was an act of worship. He said, "Every beauty which is seen here by persons of perception resembles more than anything else that celestial source from which we all come." The artist was saying the beauty we see through art and nature fulfills our hearts because it expresses the beauty of God Himself.

Somewhere along the way, the arts were forsaken by the church at large and given over to the world. But the Bible is full of beautiful expressions of creativity and artistic gifts. King David was a poet, singer, and musician. The temple, the Holy of Holies, the priests' garments, and even the Ark itself was dripping with beautiful imagery and expressions of God's magnificent throne room.

Humanity itself is an artistic expression. Adam was molded out of clay like a vessel on a potter's wheel, shaped and patiently built by God's own hands (Genesis 2:7). Adam's first job was to use his own creativity to name the animals (Genesis 2:19). Every human baby is a unique expression of God's image. None of them looking exactly the same. God's creativity is fresh with a brand-new, unique sunrise and sunset every day. As creatures made in God's image, how can we not use our creativity as an act of worship to honor Him?

Being creative doesn't mean you have to be artistic. You don't have to be good at music, art, or drama. What it does mean is that this life doesn't have to be boring or expressionless. You can start with the gifts God has given you, and discover exceptional ways to glorify God through the mind's creative abilities. Man is the only creature on earth with the ability to innovate and create. It is part of the image of God we bear, and God is most glorified when we use our abilities to their greatest capacity.

Ephesians 2:10 says, "For we are his workmanship, created in Christ Jesus for good works, which God prepared beforehand, that we should walk in them."

How does it challenge you to know that God created you for particular good works?

Exodus 35:31-35 describes the individuals who constructed the tabernacle, saying "…and [God] has filled him with the Spirit of God, with skill, with intelligence, with knowledge, and with all craftsmanship, to devise artistic designs, to work in gold and silver and bronze, in cutting stones for setting, and in carving wood, for work in every skilled craft … He has filled them with skill to do every sort of work done by an engraver or by a designer or by an embroiderer in blue and purple and scarlet yarns and fine twined linen, or by a weaver—by any sort of workman or skilled designer."

What does this tell you about God's idea of creativity?

First Chronicles 22:15-16 says David said to Solomon, "You have an abundance of workmen: stonecutters, masons, carpenters, and all kind of craftsmen without number, skilled in working gold, silver, bronze, and iron. Arise and work! The Lord be with you!"

What gifts and talents has God given you to use for His glory?

Read the Parable of the Talents in Matthew 25:14-30.

How does this parable apply to the gifts God has given each person?

Edith Schaeffer wrote, "Constructive creativity not only affects other human beings, but brings glory to God by being in the stream of His creativity."

How does this inspire you?

In his book *Inside Out Worship*, Matt Redman wrote, "Creativity is essential when it comes to our congregational worship. It's a sign of abundant life."

How do your gifts contribute to the abundant life?

God's handiwork is seen throughout nature. Look out your window.

How do you see the creativity of God in nature?

"Name it and claim it" teaching (aka, the prosperity gospel), has often been criticized for its focus on material blessings. And that criticism certainly has its rightful place. Jesus said, "Do not lay up for yourselves treasures on earth, where moth and rust destroy and where thieves break in and steal" (Matthew 6:19). The Apostle Paul said, "Those who desire to be rich fall into temptation, into a snare, into many senseless and harmful desires that plunge people into ruin and destruction" (1 Timothy 6:9). Clearly, the Bible does not encourage accumulating carnal possessions.

But the Bible often mentions heavenly rewards. Should Christians serve with these rewards in mind? Yes. Jesus cautioned against earthly treasures, but He immediately encouraged accumulating heavenly treasures saying, "… Lay up for yourselves treasures in heaven, where neither moth nor rust destroys and where thieves do not break in and steal. For where your treasure is, there your heart will be also" (Matthew 6:20-21).

The work and sacrifices we make for the kingdom will not go unnoticed. Paul said, "… Each will receive his wages according to his labor" (1 Corinthians 3:8). And Jesus said when we do good, even when no one is looking, "your Father who sees in secret will reward you" (Matthew 6:4).

God loves to give gifts to His people. Like any loving Father, He enjoys giving you the desires of your heart. Jesus encouraged us to ask God for anything according to His will in prayer. He said, "If you then, who are evil, know how to give good gifts to your children, how much more will your Father who is in heaven give good things to those who ask him!" (Matthew 7:7-11).

Our treasures are not of this world, but the Christian life is one that promises reward. God is abundantly generous, and He has promised to share His majestic wealth with His heirs. Don't be afraid to long for that day when you finally see "your labor is not in vain" (1 Corinthians 15:58).

C. S. Lewis wrote, "Aim at Heaven and you will get earth 'thrown in': aim at earth and you will get neither."

What do you think Lewis meant by that?

Mother Teresa said, "Our life of poverty is as necessary as the work itself. Only in heaven will we see how much we owe to the poor for helping us to love God better because of them."

How does this quote challenge you?

Jesus said, "For the Son of Man is going to come with his angels in the glory of his Father, and then he will repay each person according to what he has done" (Matthew 16:27)

How does this scripture make you feel?

First Corinthians 2:9 says, "What no eye has seen, nor ear heard, nor the heart of man imagined, what God has prepared for those who love him."

Meditate on this verse, and write about your thoughts.

Think about the good things you have done for the kingdom.

Write about the ones that might bring reward in heaven.

Pray and thank God for His abundance in gifts and rewards.

Ask Him to give you the incentive and courage to do more.

Read the Parable of the Talents again in Matthew 25:14-30.

What do you learn about reward from Jesus' teaching?

Made in the USA
Lexington, KY
18 November 2019